Stitch-by-Stitch

Stitch-by-Stitch

A handy step-by-step guide

Jane Bull

DK

LONDON, NEW YORK, MELBOURNE, MUNICH, DELHI

Project Editor Katharine Goddard
Senior Art Editor Elaine Hewson
Managing Editor Penny Smith
Senior Managing Art Editor Marianne Markham
Producer, Pre-Production Rebecca Fallowfield
Senior Producer Katherine Whyte
Special Sales Creative Project Manager Alison Donovan

DK INDIA

Editors Janashree Singha, Manasvi Vohra
Senior Art Editor Balwant Singh
Art Editor Zaurin Thoidingjam
Assistant Art Editor Nikita Sodhi
DTP Designer Satish Chandra Gaur

First published in Great Britain in 2014
by Dorling Kindersley Limited
80 Strand, London WC2R 0RL

Material in this publication was previously published in:
Stitch-by-Stitch (2011) and Made by Me (2013)

A Penguin Random House Company

This edition produced for The Book People Ltd,
Hall Wood Avenue, Haydock, St Helens, WA11 9UL

A CIP catalogue record for this book is available
from the British Library

ISBN 978-1-4093-6965-3

Printed and bound in China by Leo Paper Products Ltd.

Discover more at **www.dk.com/crafts**

This book's for my needlecraft teacher Barbara Owen (who's also my mum).

Crochet

Stitch-by-Stitch

is all about needlecraft,

introducing beginners to embroidery, crochet, patchwork, appliqué, knitting, and needlepoint. It teaches the basic techniques and then takes them a step further, showing how to use the new skills to create fun and beautiful projects, revitalizing the skills our grandmothers took for granted and bringing them up to date.

Embroidery

Patchwork

Knitting

Needlepoint

Appliqué

Contents

Keep your sewing essentials in little boxes.

SOFT-TOY FILLING is used for stuffing projects such as patchwork balls, cushions, and knitted dolls. It is a lightweight material that gives an even stuffing.

FELT is available in lots of colours. It's easy to cut into small shapes and is a useful backing material.

Felt is perfect for projects because the edges don't fray.

RIBBONS and braids are great for decorating projects, so keep a selection in your sewing box.

Keep to hand

Here is a selection of equipment and materials that will come in handy when making the projects in this book.

Self-covering DIY buttons can be bought in craft shops.

Safety pins to make brooches

Brightly coloured buttons

PINKING SHEARS are special scissors with zig-zag-shaped blades that make a shape when cutting fabric. The zig-zag edge prevents the material from fraying.

COTTON FABRIC is lightweight and can be used for embroidery projects, appliqué, or patchwork.

A button box

Sewing basics

All the projects in Stitch-by-Stitch will need a handy kit like this, as well as the materials and equipment required for a particular technique. You will also need to know some basic sewing skills to complete the projects.

Sewing box

You can buy a sewing box to store all your sewing equipment and materials, but why not make one out of a shoebox instead?

Handy tip

Remember to keep this kit with you when making the projects in this book.

Thread

It's handy to have a selection of sewing threads in different colours so you can match them to the fabrics you use. Needle threaders are useful.

Needles

Sewing needles are usually thin with either a small eye or a long, thin eye. Keep a selection of needles in a needle case.

Pins

You'll need pins in a lot of the sewing projects. A pincushion keeps your pins safe and always at hand. Glass-headed pins are pretty and easy to see when dropped.

SEWING THREAD

NEEDLE THREADER

EMBROIDERY SCISSORS

NEEDLE CASE

DRESSMAKERS' SCISSORS

PINCUSHION

THIMBLE

TAPE MEASURE

Scissors

It helps to have good sharp scissors and the right ones for the job. Embroidery scissors are best for snipping threads and dressmakers' scissors are best for cutting larger pieces of fabric.

Thimble

You wear a thimble on the middle finger of the hand that is holding the needle. It is used to push the needle through the fabric and stops your finger from getting sore.

Tape measure

Some projects will have thread, fabric, and yarn that need accurate measuring.

Threading a needle

Threading a needle can be difficult. A needle with a larger eye will make it easier, or use a needle threader. Use sharp scissors to cut the thread.

Thread length?

If you work with thread that is too long it will get tangled, slowing you down. Cut a piece of thread roughly the length from your fingers to your elbow.

Thread the needle.

Double up the thread and knot the end.

The eye of the needle

Large eye

Cut the end of the thread with sharp scissors.

Push the thread through the eye of the needle.

USING A NEEDLE THREADER

1. Push the threader wire through the eye of the needle. ....

2. Put the end of the thread though the wire. ....

Pull the wire and thread through the eye.

Remove the wire.

Sewing on a button

1

First secure the thread in the fabric. Then put the button onto the needle and drop it down the thread.

2 Push the needle back through the holes in the button. ....

3 Continue stitching up and down through the button and fabric.

4 To secure the button bring the thread up under the button. ....

Sew backwards and forwards behind the button, then cut the thread.

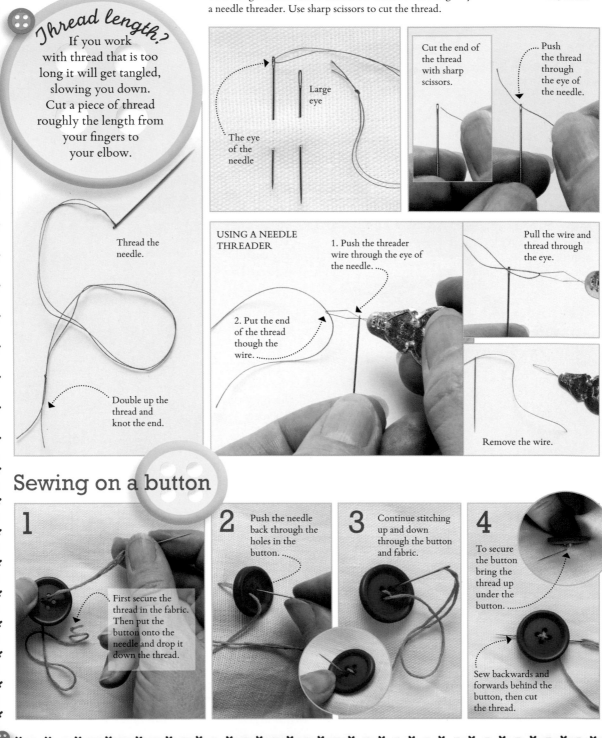

Sewing stitches

Here are the stitches that are used for the projects. They all have a different job to do when you are joining fabric together for cushions, bags, and patchwork pieces.

How to start and finish

Begin stitching with a knot at the end of the thread. To end a row of stitches, make a tiny stitch, but do not pull it tight. Bring the thread back up through the loop and pull tight. Do this once more in the same spot, then cut the thread.

Running stitch

Keep the stitch and the spaces between them small and even.

This is a very versatile stitch used for seams, joining fabric together, and for gathering.

Back stitch

This is the strongest stitch. It makes a continuous line of stitches so it is best for joining two pieces of fabric securely, like the sides of a bag.

Make the stitch then bring the needle back to the place where the last stitch is finished.

Bring the needle out ready to begin the next stitch.

VIEW FROM REVERSE

Tacking stitch

Tacking stitches are like running stitches but are larger and don't need to be even.

This is a temporary stitch. It will be removed but it is useful for holding pieces of fabric in place before you sew them together properly. It is also known as basting stitch.

Overstitch

Insert the needle diagonally from the back of the fabric.

Pick up only two or three threads of fabric.

These are tiny, neat, and even stitches that are almost invisible. Use them to top sew two finished edges together, such as when you are joining patchwork pieces.

Slip stitch

Slide the needle into the fold of the fabric.

Use slip stitch when you want the stitches to be invisible. This stitch is made by slipping the thread under a fold of fabric. It is often used to join two folded edges, such as the openings of cushions.

Bring the needle out then slide the needle in the other side.

Embroidery

Needlework embroidery is the handicraft of decorating fabric or other materials with a needle and thread. With a variety of stitches it's possible to create beautiful pictures and patterns.

Plain-weave fabric

Any kind of fabric can be used for embroidery stitches. Here are examples of cotton, linen, and felt. These fabrics are ideal for freestyle embroidery.

Cotton and linen fabric

Embroidery needle

Tapestry needle

Cotton gingham

Felt

Even-weave fabric

These fabrics are designed especially for embroidery. Woven from cotton, the square mesh produces regular stitches. They are gauged by the count or number of threads to every 2.5cm (1in). The more threads, the finer the fabric.

8-count Binca

14-count Aida cloth

Needles and threads

The two types of needle used in the projects are embroidery for fine fabric and tapestry.

Embroidery threads are made up of six strands which can be separated. Finer fabric will require fewer strands.

13cm (5in) hoop

Embroidery thread

8cm (3in) hoop

Hoops

Embroidery hoops are round frames that come in small and large sizes. Flimsy fabric can be clamped tight so it's easier to work on.

Designs on even-weave fabric

Here is an example to show how the different counted thread affects the design. Notice how the same motif, using the same amount of stitches, changes size.

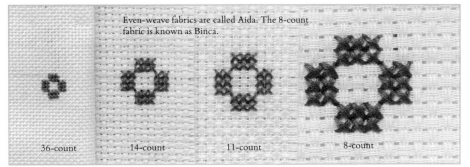

Even-weave fabrics are called Aida. The 8-count fabric is known as Binca.

36-count   14-count   11-count   8-count

Transferring designs

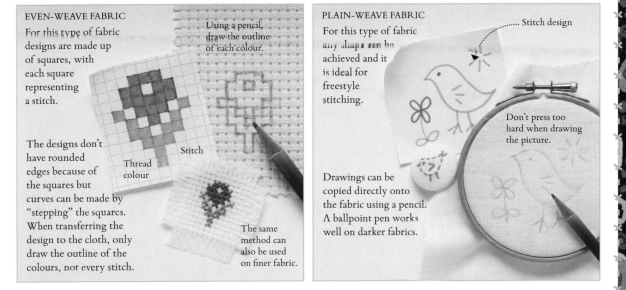

EVEN-WEAVE FABRIC

For this type of fabric designs are made up of squares, with each square representing a stitch.

The designs don't have rounded edges because of the squares but curves can be made by "stepping" the squares. When transferring the design to the cloth, only draw the outline of the colours, not every stitch.

Using a pencil, draw the outline of each colour.

Thread colour

Stitch

The same method can also be used on finer fabric.

PLAIN-WEAVE FABRIC

For this type of fabric any shape can be achieved and it is ideal for freestyle stitching.

Drawings can be copied directly onto the fabric using a pencil. A ballpoint pen works well on darker fabrics.

Stitch design

Don't press too hard when drawing the picture.

How to use a hoop

Tension screw to adjust the outer ring

Hoops are made in two parts. The inner ring is solid and the outer ring is adjustable.

Lay the fabric centrally over the inner ring.

Tighten the screw to hold the fabric.

Gently push the outer ring over the fabric, keeping the fabric straight.

Stitches gallery

Running stitch

This stitch makes a dashed line. The stitches can vary in length depending on the effect you want.

Make stitches by bringing the needle in and out. ⋯

Back stitch

Back stitch creates a continuous line.

Make a stitch then place the needle back in where it started. ⋯

Pull the needle through.

Place the needle to make another stitch and repeat the first step.

Cross stitch

'X' stitches can be worked in a row or on their own.

Stitch diagonal stitches in the same direction.

Bring the needle out here ready to begin the next stitch.

To complete the 'X' shapes, work back across the row, using the same hole as the previous stitch.

Blanket stitch

This stitch is perfect for edging projects and for decoration.

Bring the needle out and back into the fabric.

Keep the thread under the needle.

Place the needle back ready to make the next stitch.

Prepare the needle for the next stitch.

Repeat the steps to complete a line of stitches.

Chain stitch

A decorative stitch with a chain effect.

Single chains can look like leaves or petals.

Bring the needle out and then put it back in next to the first stitch.

Pull the thread through until it forms a loop.

Bring the needle back up just inside the loop.

Push the needle back in next to the last stitch.

Make a new loop and repeat the steps to continue making a chain.

Crown stitch

A decorative stitch

Bring the thread round to form a loose stitch.

Make a stitch over the stitch to hold it in place.

Continue making stitches.

A third stitch completes the crown stitch.

French knot

You can make all sorts of patterns with these little knots.

Wind the thread twice around the needle.

Push the needle back in close to the first stitch.

Pull the needle through to form the knot.

Handy tip

Cut a length of thread that is about the length from your fingertips to your elbow to avoid tangles and knots in the thread.

Threading a needle

Tapestry needle   Embroidery needle

Separate out the six strands.

To separate the six strands, hold three strands with one hand and slide the other hand down the length of the thread.

1. To thread three or six strands of thread, loop the thread over the needle and pull tight.

2. Bring the eye of the needle over the thread.

3. Pull the thread through the eye of the needle.

Starting and stopping

STARTING OFF

Knot the thread and bring it up through the fabric.

Hold the hoop in one hand and use the other to sew the design.

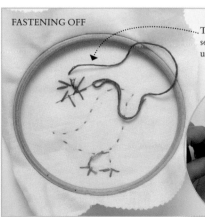

FASTENING OFF

Turn the work over. To secure the thread, pass it under the stitches nearby.

Cut the thread off.

Just by using simple stitches like blanket stitch, chain stitch, and straight stitch you can make really colourful designs.

Felt flowers

To make a bunch of flowers save all those pretty scraps of felt and transform them into bright and cheery blooms. Play with the colours of the felt and thread for dazzling effects.

You will need
• Colourful felt scraps
• Embroidery thread
• Embroidery needle

Small lengths of embroidery thread

Save small pieces of felt for projects like this.

Attaching a pin to the back of the flower makes a charming brooch.

Flower templates

Place tracing paper on top of these shapes and trace over them with pencil. Transfer the design onto thin card. Cut out the card and use the shapes for the felt flower.

See page 60 for transferring designs.

See page 62 for templates.

Pictures in stitches

Big and small, you can make the same picture in a different size by using a different counted-thread fabric.

Make a picture

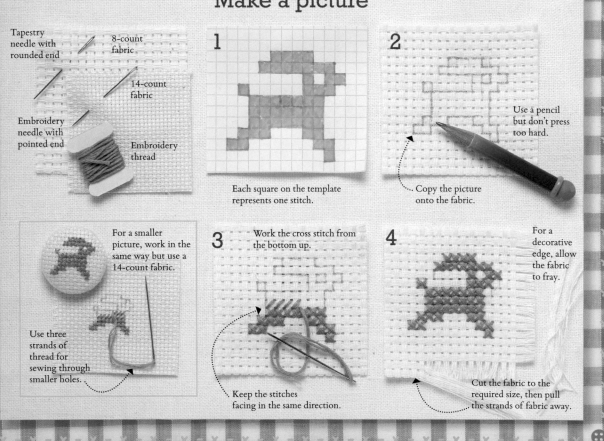

Tapestry needle with rounded end

8-count fabric

14-count fabric

Embroidery needle with pointed end

Embroidery thread

1 Each square on the template represents one stitch.

2 Use a pencil but don't press too hard.

Copy the picture onto the fabric.

For a smaller picture, work in the same way but use a 14-count fabric.

Use three strands of thread for sewing through smaller holes.

3 Work the cross stitch from the bottom up.

Keep the stitches facing in the same direction.

4 For a decorative edge, allow the fabric to fray.

Cut the fabric to the required size, then pull the strands of fabric away.

Glue your
picture to
the front of
greeting
cards.

See pages 20-21 for
making buttons.

DIY key fob
from craft shop

There are lots of ways that you
can use your pictures, from
greeting cards to buttons, box lids
to key fobs – just perfect as gifts.

Customize your stuff
by attaching different-
sized pictures to your
belongings. Create a
matching set instantly!

Beautiful buttons

Like precious gems, covering these button bases with your work can make even the tiniest piece of embroidery look special. What a perfect way to use up scrap fabric and short ends of thread. Sew to your clothes to replace your buttons or wear as a brooch.

You will need

Scraps of fabric

Leftover embroidery threads

Sewing thread

Sewing needle

Embroidery needle

Button template for fabric size

Button base top and bottom

How to make a button

1 Cut a piece of fabric larger than the button template.

Begin your embroidery in the centre.

2 Draw around the card template.

Cut out the fabric.

3 Sew around the edge of the fabric.

Running stitch

Sewing needle and thread

4 Place the button top in the centre of the fabric.

Gently pull the thread to gather the fabric.

5 Secure the fabric by sewing backwards and forwards.

6 Press the back of the button down firmly.

Felt flower design
(See pages 16–17).

Stitch over the designs
on printed fabric.

Cross-stitch motifs
(see pages 18–19).

Buttons galore

Experiment with the embroidery you have tried with the other projects on the previous pages. These small areas are great for practicing your skills.

Needlepoint

Also known as tapestry, or canvas work, needlepoint is the craft of stitching onto a firm open-weave canvas. The stitches are worked on a canvas grid and tightly stitched so that none of the background is left showing.

Large eye

Tapestry needles

Rounded end

Needles

Also known as tapestry needles, needlepoint needles have rounded ends. This helps to prevent the point from catching the canvas threads. The large eye makes it easy to thread.

Canvas

Canvas is made of cotton thread that has been treated to make it very stiff. It is sized by mesh sizes, or thread count per 2.5cm (1in); for example "10 count" means there are 10 threads to 2.5cm (1in). The sizes range from 5 count to 24 count; the smaller the mesh, the finer the stitches will be. Canvas can be bought with a pre-printed design in kits from craft shops, or plain in metre lengths.

The projects in this book use 10-count canvas – 10 threads to 2.5cm (1in)

Skeins of tapestry wool

Projects

There are all kinds of needlepoint equipment and materials available, from plastic canvas to kits with printed designs. The items shown here are all you need to complete the projects that follow and to create your own designs too.

Threads

Needlepoint thread comes in wool, cotton, or silk. Tapestry wool gives the best results on 10-count canvas, as the woollen stitches lay close together, completely hiding the canvas underneath. You can buy it in measured lengths called skeins.

Cutting the canvas

Taping the edges is optional.

Before you start, cut out a piece of canvas. Count the number of stitches required for your design and then decide how much room to leave around the edge, as the canvas needs to be larger than your design. This border can be cut away later or kept if you want to frame your work.

The image area

If the wool keeps catching on the edge of the canvas, use masking tape to cover the edges.

Masking tape

Transferring designs

(See the project pages for designs as well as the templates on pages 60–61.)

Needlepoint designs are made up of squares, with each square representing a stitch. Notice that the stitch doesn't go in the holes of the canvas but across the threads. The design is just a guide. Create your own design or use one of the templates in this book.

Design your own image on squared paper.

Squared paper

Copy the design onto the canvas, colouring the places the stitches will go.

NOTE: See where the stitches go.

Threading a tapestry needle

Cut a piece of wool 50cm (20in) long, thread the needle, and knot the end of the wool.

Fold the end of the wool over the needle and pull tight.

Pinch the loop between your fingers.

Put the eye of the needle over the loop.

Slide the eye of the needle down the loop.

Pull the wool through until the short end is out of the eye.

Begin stitching

These steps have been made using tent stitch.

Push the needle from the front to the back so the knot is on the front.

Waste knot.

Bring the needle back up through the canvas and begin the first stitch.

Continue stitching the same colour forwards and backwards.

Keep the stitch facing in the same direction.

To finish a colour, turn the work over and slide the needle under the stitches.

Pull the needle all the way through and then cut off the wool.

Add new colour

To begin a new colour slide the needle under a row of stitches.

Pull the needle all the way through.

Continue stitching in the new colour as before.

Finish the colour, turn the work over, and slide the needle under the stitches.

Continue as before.

Finishing off

Continue stitching the design following the pattern.

To complete the stitching, fasten off the last colour.

The waste knot is now secure under the stitches.

The waste knot can now be cut off.

Needlepoint stitches

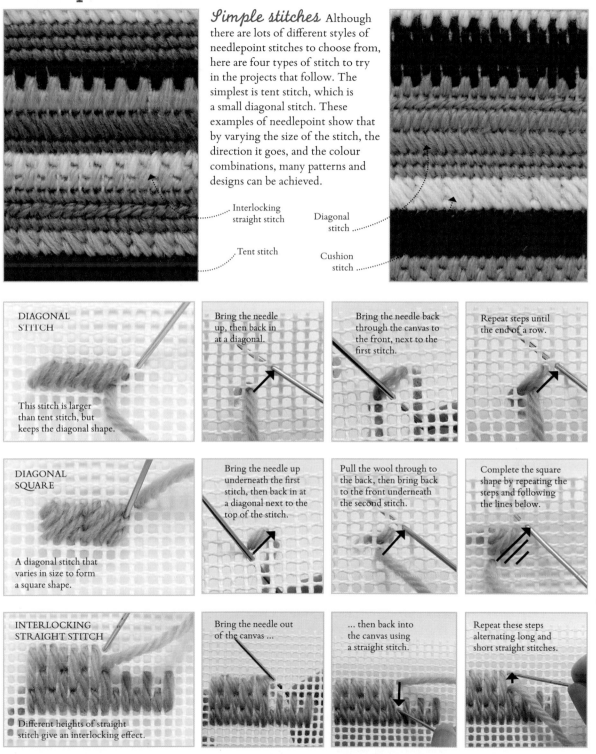

Simple stitches Although there are lots of different styles of needlepoint stitches to choose from, here are four types of stitch to try in the projects that follow. The simplest is tent stitch, which is a small diagonal stitch. These examples of needlepoint show that by varying the size of the stitch, the direction it goes, and the colour combinations, many patterns and designs can be achieved.

Interlocking straight stitch

Tent stitch

Diagonal stitch

Cushion stitch

DIAGONAL STITCH

This stitch is larger than tent stitch, but keeps the diagonal shape.

Bring the needle up, then back in at a diagonal.

Bring the needle back through the canvas to the front, next to the first stitch.

Repeat steps until the end of a row.

DIAGONAL SQUARE

A diagonal stitch that varies in size to form a square shape.

Bring the needle up underneath the first stitch, then back in at a diagonal next to the top of the stitch.

Pull the wool through to the back, then bring back to the front underneath the second stitch.

Complete the square shape by repeating the steps and following the lines below.

INTERLOCKING STRAIGHT STITCH

Different heights of straight stitch give an interlocking effect.

Bring the needle out of the canvas ...

... then back into the canvas using a straight stitch.

Repeat these steps alternating long and short straight stitches.

Stripy pouch

Here's a chance to try out a variety of stitches and play with colours. Create simple stripy designs to decorate these handy little pouches – they're great for storing music players.

You will need

- 10-count canvas
- Tapestry wool in various colours • Tapestry needle
- Felt fabric • Sewing needle and thread

1 Cut the canvas larger than the finished pouch size.

Canvas size 7cm (3in) x 12cm (5in)

Pouch size 5cm (2in) x 10cm (4in)

Begin stitching at the base of the canvas and work upwards.

2 Use a pencil to mark out the area to be stitched.

Continue until the stitch area is filled.

Change stitch style and colour as you move up.

3 Carefully cut around the canvas.

Don't cut too close or the canvas will come apart.

Stitch over the edge of the canvas.

Continue all the way around the edge.

5 Cut the felt the same size as the canvas work.

Stitch the two pieces together leaving an opening at the top.

Sewing needle and thread

Gadget pouch

Perfect for keeping your phone or music player safely tucked away – you can use it for glasses too.

Measure up
Decide what the pouch will be used for, like your music player for example. Measure its height and width – don't forget how thick it is too and include this in the width otherwise the pouch will be too tight.

7cm (3in) x 12cm (5in)

Sewing pouch

Perfect for sewing essentials, such as small, sharp embroidery scissors.

5cm (2in) x 10cm (4in)

7cm (3in) x 12cm (5in)

Patchwork

To make patchwork, small shaped pieces of fabric are sewn together in geometric patterns to create a large patterned cloth – a perfect way to reuse scraps and recycle clothes.

Paper for patches

Each fabric patch will need to be attached to a paper shape. You can reuse old envelopes and magazines to make these. You will need a lot as each patch has its own piece of paper, but they can be reused when the project is finished.

Patchwork fabric

Light-weight cotton is best for patchwork; don't use anything stretchy or too thick as it'll be difficult to make the patches even. Experiment with colours and patterns too.

Isometric paper to create designs (see templates on page 60)

Tracing paper

Old envelopes are good for paper patches.

Graph paper for patch designs

Sewing needle and pins

Sewing thread for tacking fabric to paper patches and for sewing patches together

Card for templates

Ruler for drawing and measuring templates

Card templates

Card from cereal boxes is ideal, but any card that is easy to cut out will do.

Pencil to draw round the shapes

How patchwork works

Every patch needs a piece of fabric and a paper shape. The paper is tacked to the fabric, and then these patches are stitched together. The paper remains in the patch until you have finished. Templates made out of card are used to get the right size for the fabric and paper.

| Square | Pentagon | Hexagon | Triangle |

Patchwork pieces are based on these shapes.

Copy the shape for the template onto tracing paper using a pencil (see page 60 for templates).

Turn the tracing paper over and lay it on the card.

Scribble over the back of the pencil line.

The pencil line will have transferred onto the card.

Card templates

Cut out the card shapes.

The large shape is for the fabric.

The smaller shape is for the paper.

Preparing the paper shapes

1

Carefully draw around the card edge.

2

Cut out the paper shapes.

It's important to draw and cut the shapes accurately, because they will determine the shape of your final patch.

Preparing the fabric

Select some fabrics that work well together.

Use the large card template for the fabric.

2

Draw around the edge of the card (NOTE: a ballpoint pen works well on fabric).

3

Cut out the fabric shapes.

Preparing the patches

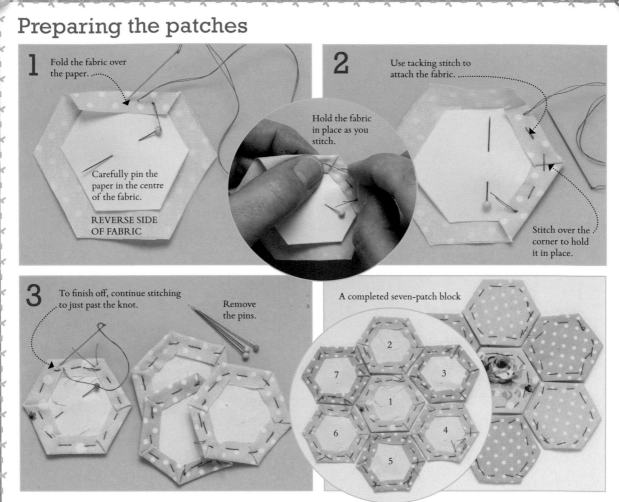

1 Fold the fabric over the paper.

Carefully pin the paper in the centre of the fabric.

REVERSE SIDE OF FABRIC

Hold the fabric in place as you stitch.

2 Use tacking stitch to attach the fabric.

Stitch over the corner to hold it in place.

3 To finish off, continue stitching to just past the knot.

Remove the pins.

A completed seven-patch block

Sewing patches together

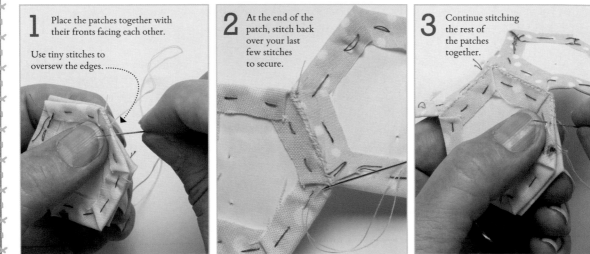

1 Place the patches together with their fronts facing each other.

Use tiny stitches to oversew the edges.

2 At the end of the patch, stitch back over your last few stitches to secure.

3 Continue stitching the rest of the patches together.

Removing the paper patch

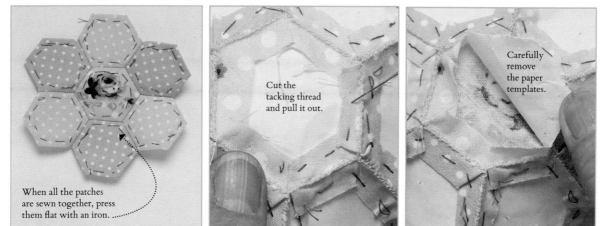

When all the patches are sewn together, press them flat with an iron.

Cut the tacking thread and pull it out.

Carefully remove the paper templates.

Pressing the patch

Once the paper has been removed, the patches are quite flimsy and the folded seams will tend to unfold. To keep them in shape, press with a hot iron.

Press the back when the paper is removed.

Save the paper shapes as they are reusable.

Use a cotton cloth to protect the front when pressing.

Patchwork pattern blocks

Triangles can be used to make up blocks of larger triangles or squares.

Blocks When patches are sewn together like this they are known as blocks. These blocks can help when making large pieces. Placing the blocks in different ways creates all sorts of new designs.

Six-sided shapes, sewn together, make a seven-patch block.

Squares can be joined to make a nine-patch block.

Squares and triangles

Lots of patterns can be made by placing blocks of triangles in different ways. Choose fabrics with very different contrasting colours and patterns for more dramatic effects.

Make a block

Make four triangular patches using the template on page 60. Try using the squared graph paper.

Pin the paper template in the centre of the fabric.

Fold the fabric over the paper and sew in place.

You will need

• 4 different fabric designs • Paper templates (see page 60) • Sewing thread and needle

Make four triangles the same size.

Stitch the triangles together.

Fold down all the pointed ends and pin them along the folded edge. Neatly sew all round the edge.

Make three more blocks in the same way.

Sew the four blocks together on the reverse side using small stitches.

Join blocks together

Turn each block around so the triangles match up differently.

Remove the paper and use an iron to press the reverse side flat.

Project idea

This design has been used to decorate a cushion. Place the block design centrally on the cushion and neatly sew it on. If you sew lots of blocks together you can make a big floor cushion.

Patchy cushions

Shaped like a honeycomb, these six-sided patches are sewn together to make a seven-patch block. Here two blocks have been stitched together and stuffed to make cushions.

Make 2 x seven-patch blocks

To make the blocks follow the steps on pages 28–31.

This design uses a different fabric for each patch.

To help flatten the fabric, iron the blocks before removing the paper.

How to make a pincushion

1 Remove the template paper.

... Iron the fabric edges flat again at this stage.

2 Place the blocks with the wrong sides facing each other.

Neatly oversew the edges together.

Leave an opening for the filling.

3 Fill the cushion, working the stuffing into the corners. ...

Neatly sew up the opening.

Little and large

It's so simple; the size of the patch will make a smaller or larger cushion. Go to page 60 and try out some different sized templates.

Match the patch

The seven-patch blocks can be sewn together to become a larger piece of fabric, such as a quilt for your bed.

Appliqué

What is appliqué? Well, it's pictures and patterns made by sewing small fabric shapes to a piece of material. Motifs can be used like patches to dress up clothing. Sewing stitches can be invisible but embroidery stitches are a perfect way to add decoration.

Fabrics

Light-weight cotton fabric is best for appliqué. As well as coming in an array of colours and patterns, it is easy to cut and shape. The cut edges will fray but stitching the edges and using adhesive transfer paper will help. Avoid stretchy fabric as this can distort the motif shapes.

Tracing paper

Use this for copying an image and transferring the outline as a pattern for your piece of fabric.

Transfer paper

Used in dress making and craft projects, this paper has a glued backing that, when heated, can be used to attach motifs to the fabric items.

Buttons for decoration

Tracing paper

Transfer paper

Embroidery thread

Needles and pins

Sewing thread

Scissors for cutting out shapes

Pencil for tracing motifs

Felt fabric

Felt will not fray like other fabrics because of the way it is made. This makes it ideal for appliqué as even the smallest motifs will keep their shape.

Transferring designs using transfer paper

What is transfer paper?

Transfer paper is a handy way to attach motifs to the fabric items you want to decorate. It's like tracing paper with glue on one side. It works in two steps; first you stick the paper shape to your motif fabric and then you iron the motif to the fabric you are decorating. Use the maker's instructions.

1 Place the transfer paper over the image you have chosen and trace over the outline with a pencil.

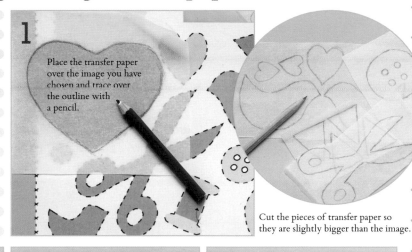

Cut the pieces of transfer paper so they are slightly bigger than the image.

2 Carefully cut along the line.

3 Place the paper shape on the wrong side of the fabric.

Gently iron over the paper shape until it is fixed in place.

4 Carefully cut around the paper shape.

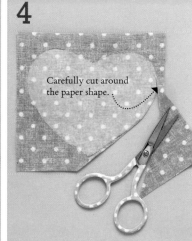

5 Peel away the backing paper.

Now turn over the motif so the right side is facing up.

6 Carefully position the motif where you want it to go.

Gently iron all over the motif until it is stuck down.

Using an iron

- The iron will need to be hot to make the transfer paper work effectively.

- PLEASE NOTE: Some fabrics will melt if you iron them. Place a piece of cotton cloth over the fabric motif before ironing to prevent this happening.

Paper patterns

Fabric motifs can be attached by simply pinning them directly to the base fabric. Trace over the image and cut out the shape, then using the tracing-paper shape, cut out the fabric motif.

Tracing paper template

Using tracing paper and a pencil, draw the outline of the motif.

Cut out the shape.

Carefully cut around the paper.

Pin the tracing-paper pattern to the right side of the fabric.

Pin the fabric shape in postion on the base material.

Decorative stitching

Stitches used for attaching the motifs can be tiny and invisible, using sewing thread, or they can be made to be part of the design. Try using the stitches from the Embroidery pages of the book (pages 12–19). Here are three decorative ways of making stitches part of the design using embroidery thread.

RUNNING STITCH

STRAIGHT STITCH

BLANKET STITCH

This stitch is useful if the edges of fabric are fraying.

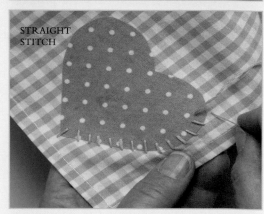

Ready-made motifs

Look out for fabric with big, bold designs because these make perfect motifs.

DIY shapes

Design your own motifs. If you can't find a design you like or you have a picture in mind, draw the design on paper and use this as your pattern. Cut out the shapes and pin them to the fabric, then cut out to make the fabric shapes.

Handy tip

If you don't have any adhesive transfer paper, simply cut out the shapes, pin them to the backing material, and sew them in place.

Iron the paper on the reverse of the fabric, over the motif.

Cut out the motif.

Iron the motif in position.

Cup-cake bag

Create a delicious cup-cake bag made of felt and buttons. First draw your design on paper, then cut it out to use as the pattern. Felt is great because it doesn't fray at the edges.

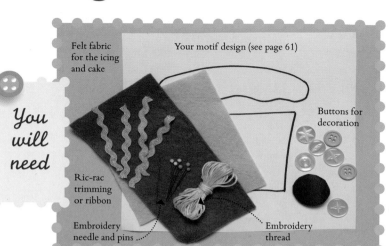

You will need

Felt fabric for the icing and cake

Your motif design (see page 61)

Buttons for decoration

Ric-rac trimming or ribbon

Embroidery needle and pins

Embroidery thread

Bag size

Cut out a piece of fabric 20cm (8in) x 42cm (16in). Position the motif in the top half of the fabric, as shown below. Remember to allow space for the seams and for turning over at the top of the bag.

Fold over edges at the top of bag.

Fold line

Back of the bag

Side seams

How to make the motif

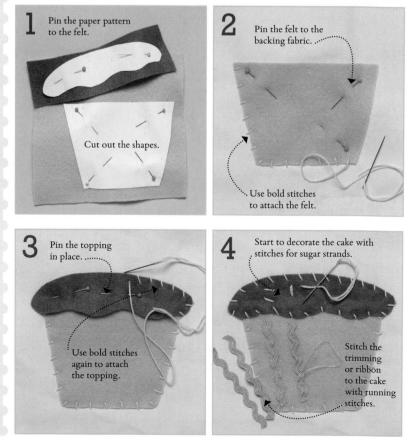

1 Pin the paper pattern to the felt.

Cut out the shapes.

2 Pin the felt to the backing fabric.

Use bold stitches to attach the felt.

3 Pin the topping in place.

Use bold stitches again to attach the topping.

4 Start to decorate the cake with stitches for sugar strands.

Stitch the trimming or ribbon to the cake with running stitches.

Ready-made

If you already have a bag, why not decorate that instead? Just follow the motif step-by-steps in the same way.

Use trimming or ribbon to look like the sides of a cake case.

Collect up buttons to decorate your work.

Make a bag

Fold the fabric in half, right sides facing. Fold the tops of the bag over and stitch in place on either side. Sew together the sides using back stitch. Finally, pin the handles on and sew them in position.

Fold over the fabric at the top and sew up the sides.

Pin the handles to the bag and sew them in place.

Needle case

Keep all your needles and pins at hand in a simple cloth case. This design helps you practise your sewing skills – sewing buttons and appliqué.

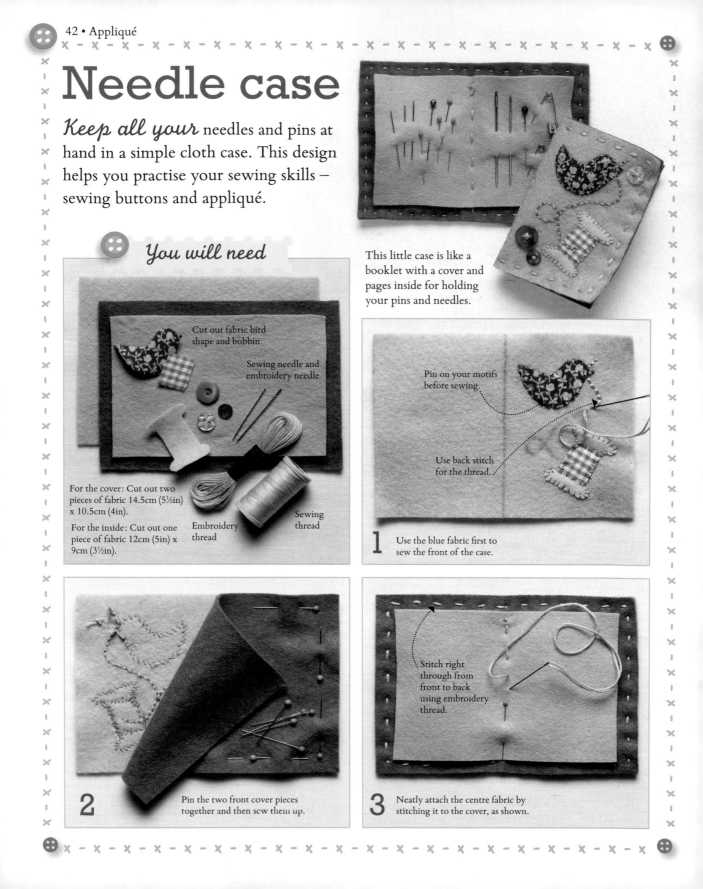

You will need

Cut out fabric bird shape and bobbin.

Sewing needle and embroidery needle

Embroidery thread

Sewing thread

For the cover: Cut out two pieces of fabric 14.5cm (5½in) x 10.5cm (4in).

For the inside: Cut out one piece of fabric 12cm (5in) x 9cm (3½in).

This little case is like a booklet with a cover and pages inside for holding your pins and needles.

Pin on your motifs before sewing.

Use back stitch for the thread.

1 Use the blue fabric first to sew the front of the case.

2 Pin the two front cover pieces together and then sew them up.

Stitch right through from front to back using embroidery thread.

3 Neatly attach the centre fabric by stitching it to the cover, as shown.

Knitting

Two needles and a ball of yarn are all you need to get knitting. Work the stitches from one needle to the other and see the fabric grow.

KNITTING RULES
There are no set rules about how to use the yarn and needle – knitters all round the world use them in quite different ways. The following pages show two methods, one of which is preferred by left-handers.

Knitting needles

Knitting needles are available in many different sizes, from very narrow ones for fine work to very thick ones that produce a chunky knit. The projects that follow use a medium-sized needle.

Tapestry needle for sewing up projects

Knitting spool

Also known as a Knitting Nancy and French Knitting, this gadget knits yarn into long braids that can be used with all kinds of projects.

The pin is used to work the yarn over the top of hooks on the spool.

4mm knitting needles

Stitch types

There are two stitch types used in the projects that follow 'Knit stitch' and 'Purl stitch'. Knitting patterns shorten the names as shown below:

K = knit

P = purl

st = stitch

Braids made with the knitting spool

"Double knit" (DK) yarn

Yarns

The many different types of yarn are described by their 'weight'. The yarn used for the projects that follow is a "Double knit" or DK weight and made of either wool or acrylic. Other yarns are known as 4-ply and chunky. Each yarn will produce a different feel to the fabric.

How to get started

Knitting is produced with two needles, one held in each hand. To begin, you need to make stitches – this is called "casting on". You will need to cast on the number of stitches required in the pattern. The stitches that are being worked will be on the left hand needle and the ones you have made will go on the right.

These loops are called stitches.

Ball of yarn

Knitted rows

Knitting needle

Slip knot The first stitch on the needle is knotted so the yarn stays on.

Loop the end of the yarn around your finger tips.

Push the yarn through the loop with your finger.

Pull the yarn through to make a loop.

Slide the new loop onto the needle.

Pull on the ball end of the yarn to tighten the loop.

Casting on There are many ways to cast on. This method uses your thumb.

1 Wrap the yarn around your thumb as shown.

2 Pick up the yarn with the needle.

3 Let the yarn go from your thumb onto the needle.

4 Continue doing this until you have enough stitches.

Counting rows
When using a pattern that requires lots of rows, it is sometimes tricky to keep count. Either keep a note on paper and tick them off or try this handy little gadget that fits on the end of your needle.

Turn the dial for each new row.

. . . 5, 4, 3, 2, 1 stitches

Now you are ready to KNIT!

Each new row will begin with the first stitch on the right.

Knit stitch

Also called plain stitch, this stitch is generally thought to be the easiest to make and is certainly a useful basic stitch for simple projects.

For knit stitch, the right-hand needle goes to the back of the stitch.

The yarn also goes at the back.

Method 1 (This is the English method.)

1 Hold the knitting with your hands in this position.

Take the yarn around the back.

Place the needle in the back of the stitch.

2 Wrap the yarn under and round the needle from right to left.

Method 2 (This is the Continental method; it might be helpful for left-handers.)

1 Place the yarn between the fingers of your left hand.

2 Use your index finger to move the yarn.

Your middle finger and thumb are used to hold the knitting in place.

Take the yarn around the front of the needle.

Garter stitch

Garter stitch isn't an actual stitch but the name given to a piece of knitting where every row is knitted in knit stitch. The effect is bobbly on both sides.

Garter stitch is also made if you knit every row in purl stitch.

3 Pull on the yarn and move the needle from the back to the front. .....

4 The right needle is now on top of the left one and has taken the stitch with it.

5 Slide the top needle to the right. The stitch will now be transferred onto the right needle, completing the stitch.

Begin the next stitch as in step 1.

3 Bring the yarn down firmly between the needles.

4 Bring the needle with the loop of yarn to the front.

5 Take the needle with the stitch off the left hand needle.

Begin the next stitch as in step 1.

Making shapes

You can shape the knitting by adding (increasing) or taking away (decreasing) stitches. There are many different ways to do this, but here are two simple methods which you can use for the projects in this book.

INCREASE SHAPE

Two stitches have been knitted together at the beginning and end of each row.

An extra stitch has been made at the beginning and the end of each row.

DECREASE SHAPE

Make a stitch - increasing

1 Begin a knit stitch as normal.

2 Don't remove the stitch from the needle.

3 Take the right hand needle behind the left needle.

Back of stitch

4 Place the needle into the back of the stitch.

5 Bring the yarn around and knit in the normal way.

6 Pull the yarn between the needles.

7 Bring the right-hand needle to the front, carrying the new stitch with it.

8 Remove the rest of the stitch off the left-hand needle.

The new stitch

Knit two together - decreasing

1 Pick up two stitches on the needle.

Make a knit stitch as usual.

2 Bring the yarn to the front and between the needles.

3 Pull the yarn between the needles.

4 Bring the right-hand needle to the front with the new loop.

5 Slip the rest of the stitch off the left needle to complete the stitch.

Join new yarn

2 Slide the knot up the yarn to the needle.

1 Tie the new yarn to the old yarn with a loose knot.

3 Continue knitting as usual.

Knit in new colour

Here the knitting is shown on the reverse side. Join the new yarn as shown (left). To tidy up the loose ends of both colours, gather them up with the working yarn as you knit.

Casting off

1 Begin the row by knitting two stitches.

2 Pick up the first stitch with the left needle.

3 Carry this first stitch over the second stitch and over the end of the needle.

4 Repeat steps 1–3 ...

5 ... until one stitch remains. Open up the loop.

6 Cut the yarn and place the end in the loop.

7 Pull the yarn to close the loop.

Tidy away ends (Sewing in ends when adding new yarn or tidying the loose ends of finished pieces.)

Use this method when tidying joined yarn and when knitting stripes.

Sew the thread into the edge of the knitting.

Thread the end with a tapestry needle.

Bring the needle out and cut the yarn.

Use this method when tidying loose ends of finished pieces.

Thread the needle onto the loose end and sew down the side of the knitting.

Bring the needle out and cut the yarn.

x – x – x – x – x – x – x – x – x – x – x – x – x – x – x – x – x – x – x – x – x – x –

Purl stitch

It's all front with purl stitch. The yarn is worked from the front and the needle goes in the front of the stitch.

For purl stitch, the needle goes in the front of the stitch.

The yarn also goes at the front too.

Method 1 (The English method.)

1 Hold the knitting with your hands in this position.

Bring the yarn to the front.

Place the needle in the front of the stitch.

2 Take the yarn between the needles.

3 Wrap it round the needle from right to left.

Method 2 (The Continental method; left-handers might find this method helpful.)

1 Place the right hand needle in the front of the stitch.

Wind the yarn around your fingers.

2 Bring the yarn around the front of the needle.

3 Pull the yarn down with your index finger.

x – x – x – x – x – x – x – x – x – x – x – x – x – x – x – x – x – x – x – x – x – x –

Purl stitch + Knit stitch = Stocking stitch

STOCKING STITCH isn't an actual stitch at all. Instead it is made by working a knit row then a purl row, a knit row then a purl row, and so on. The result is a smooth front to the knitting and a "bobbly" back.

FRONT
The knit-stitch side

BACK
The purl-stitch side

4 Pull on the yarn and move the needle from front to back ...

5 ... taking the stitch with it. ....

6 Take the rest of the yarn off the needle to complete the stitch. .....

Begin the next stitch as in step 1.

4 Bring the right hand needle from front to back taking the yarn with it. ....

5 Pull the rest of the stitch off the needle. ..

6 Now you are ready to begin the next stitch, starting at step 1 again.

Knitted roses

Make a bunch of colourful woolly roses. These simple knitted shapes are twisted and curled to form a rose flower. It only takes a small amount of wool to make one, so it's a neat way of using up spare ends.

You will need

- 4mm knitting needles
- 5m (15ft) of yarn • Felt
- Tapestry needle
- Sewing needle and thread

Rose pattern

Cast on 32 stitches
Row 1: Knit st
Row 2: Purl st
Row 3: Knit st
Row 4: Purl st
Decrease
Row 5: knit two together to end of row = 16 st
Row 6: knit two together to end of row = 8 st
Row 7: knit two together to end of row = 4 st
Row 8: knit two together = 2 st
Cast off

How to make a rose

1 Finished knitting shown upside down.

Thread one of the ends.

Sew it into the knitting.

2 Thread the yarn end from the centre.

3 Turn over the knitting.

Twist the knitting into a tight curl to form the rose shape.

4 Sew the outer side of the curl to the back of the rose to hold it in position.

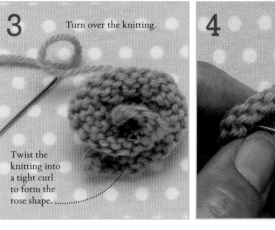

5 Cut out some felt leaves.

Sew the leaf to the back of the rose.

Overstitch the edge of the felt with small neat stitches.

Rosy brooch

Your rose makes a pretty brooch. Sew a safety pin to the felt leaves, or sew the roses directly onto your bags; either on their own or in bunches of three.

Crochet

It's all about pulling loops
through loops to create a piece of fabric,
working with only one
stitch at a time – now all you need
is a hook and some yarn.

4.5mm crochet hook

8mm crochet hook

Crochet hooks

Hooks are available in many different sizes – the larger the hook, the larger the stitch. The projects that follow are made using a medium-sized 4.5mm hook. Try using a metal hook as the yarn moves more freely compared to a plastic one.

Yarn

The projects in this book are made with cotton yarn in a double knitting (DK) weight.

This cotton yarn is not fluffy like some wools. This makes it perfect for learning how to crochet because it's easy to see the stitches.

Stitch types

When following crochet patterns the stitch names sometimes appear shortened.
Here is a guide:

ch = chain stitch; dc = double crochet (USA = single crochet); htr = half treble (USA = half double crochet); tr = treble (USA = double crochet); ss = slip stitch
Note: some patterns you find elsewhere will be based on USA names, so the results would be very different if the UK name was followed.

How to get started

Working loop

Crochet hook

Stitches

Unlike knitting, which uses two needles and where the working stitches are all on the needles, crochet is worked with a hook and only one stitch is made at one time.

Rows

This has been worked in double crochet.

HOW TO HOLD the work

Wrap the yarn around your left hand as shown here.

Hold the hook in your right hand.

Slip knot
The first stitch on the hook is knotted so the yarn stays on.

1 Make a loop with the end of the yarn around your fingertips.

2 Push the yarn through the loop with your index finger.

3 Pull the yarn through.

4 Transfer the loop onto the hook and pull gently on the yarn.

Foundation chain
The number of stitches on the chain will determine the width of the crochet fabric.

1 Hold the slip knot firmly between finger and thumb.

2 Push the hook under the yarn and catch it with the hook.

3 Pull the hook back through the stitch.

4 The stitch is complete.

NOW REPEAT STEPS 1 – 4 to continue the chain.

This foundation chain has 10 stitches – count the "V" shapes.

The back of the stitches will look very bobbly.

Make as many chain stitches as the pattern requires.

1 2 3 4 5 6 7 8 9 10

x - x - x - x - x - x - x - x - x - x - x - x - x - x - x - x - x - x - x - x - x -

Double crochet

How to start. Once you have made the foundation chain, you are ready to start crocheting. With any type of stitch you use you will need to make chain stitches at the beginning of each row so that your work is brought up to the right height.

First row in double crochet

Double crochet This basic stitch is useful for all kinds of projects. It produces a close, firm fabric.

Chain stitch At the beginning of the second row make one chain stitch. This means when you begin to work across the row you will begin at the right height.

Start with the **Foundation chain** and count the number of stitches.

10 9 8 7 6 5 4 3 2 1

2 YARN OVER
Push the hook underneath and around the yarn.

Hook the yarn and pull through the first stitch.

3 Bring the hook out.
There are now two stitches on the hook.

4 Push the hook underneath and around the yarn.
YARN OVER
Hook the yarn and pull through both stitches.

Second row in double crochet

(Use this method for all the double crochet rows from now onwards.)

1 Begin the row with a **chain stitch** so there are 11 stitches.

11

1 2 3 4 5 6 7 8 9 10

NOTE: It's always one chain stitch for double crochet.

2 YARN OVER
Push the hook under the "V" of the second stitch (10th stitch).

Hook the yarn and pull through the stitch.

3 Bring the hook out.
There are now two stitches on the hook.

x - x - x - x - x - x - x - x - x - x - x - x - x - x - x - x - x - x - x - x -

1

At the beginning of Row 1 make a **chain stitch**.

Push the hook into the centre of the 10th stitch (the second from the hook).

10

5 6 7 8 9

1 2 3 4   5   6   7   8   9   10   11

There are now 11 stitches; count the "V"s.

5

Now one stitch is left on the hook.

The **double crochet** stitch is complete.

REPEAT STEPS 1–5 to the end of the row.

10 9 8 7 6 5 4 3 2 1

The first row is complete – with 10 stitches.

Turn the work to get ready for the next row.

4

YARN OVER

Hook the yarn and pull through both stitches.

5

The stitch is complete. There is now only one stitch left on the hook.

Continue double crochet stitches to the end of the row.

10 9 8 7 6 5 4 3 2 1

Now the row is complete. Turn the work over and begin the next row and REPEAT STEPS 1–5.

Crowls

These crocheted owls or "Crowls" are made from a strip of crochet. They make cute little soft toys and even a useful addition to your sewing kit.

You will need

- Cotton yarn for eyes and body
- 4.5mm crochet hook • Soft-toy stuffing • Tapestry needle
- Sewing needle and thread

How to make owls

Small owl body

Foundation chain: 10 stitches.
First row: Make 1 chain stitch, double crochet 10 stitches.
Continue in double crochet until work measures 18cm (7in) and fasten off.

Owl eyes

Foundation chain: 2 stitches. Double crochet 10 times into the first chain stitch, slip stitch into the first double crochet stitch and fasten off.

1 Sew in the loose ends.

Fold the strip in half. Stitch the sides together.

2 Turn the work inside out.

Stuff the toy, but don't overfill.

3 Sew running stitch around the opening to close it.

Pull the thread to gather up the crochet and close the hole.

4 Sew the eye in place with a sewing needle and thread.

Handy tip

Instead of stuffing the owl you can turn it into a handy tape-measure holder. Just pop the tape measure inside and lightly stitch up the opening, checking that the tape measure can run freely in and out.

Small owl

Tape measure

Place tape measure into the opening.

Sew up the opening using overstitch.

Large owl

Foundation chain:
16 stitches.
First row: Make 1 chain stitch, double crochet 16 stitches.
Continue in double crochet until work measures 26cm (10in) and fasten off.

Templates

1 Place tracing paper over the shape and copy using a pencil.

2 Turn the tracing paper over.

Scribble over the pencil line.

3 ..The pencil line is transferred to the card.

Transferring designs

Follow steps 1–3 to transfer the patchwork designs onto paper or card.

THE BIRD AND CUP-CAKE MOTIFS Because these designs aren't symmetrical, trace the shape on both sides at step one. This way when the paper is turned over the design will be the right way round.

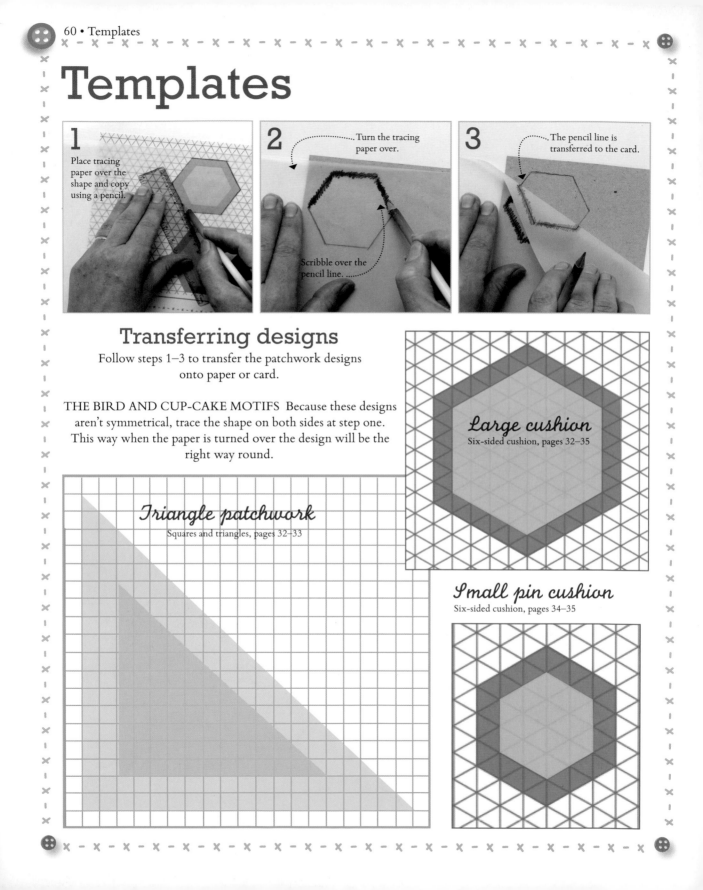

Large cushion
Six-sided cushion, pages 32–35

Triangle patchwork
Squares and triangles, pages 32–33

Small pin cushion
Six-sided cushion, pages 34–35

Cup cake

Cup-cake motif, pages 40-41

Stitching patterns

Patterns for picture stitches on pages 18-19.

Index

• A •

Aida fabric 12, 13
appliqué 36-43
    Cup-cake bag 40-41
    motifs 38, 39
    Needle case 42-43
    stitches 38

• B •

back stitch 11, 14
bags
    Cup-cake bag 40-41
    Stripy pouch 26-27
basting stitch 11
Binca fabric 13
blanket stitch 14, 38
brooches 17, 53
buttons 8
    Beautiful buttons 20-21
    self-covering 8
    sewing on a button 10

• C •

canvas 22, 23
    cutting 23
canvas work *see* needlepoint
chain stitch (crochet) 54, 55, 56
chain stitch (embroidery) 14
cotton fabric 8
crochet 54-55
    Crowls 58-59
    techniques 55-57
    yarns 54
crochet hooks 54
crochet stitches
    chain stitch 54, 55, 56
    double crochet 54, 56-57
    foundation chain 55

    half treble crochet 54
    slip knot 55
    treble crochet 54
cross stitch 14
    Pictures in stitches 18-19, 62
crown stitch 15
cushion stitch 25
cushions
    Patchy cushions 34-35, 60
Squares and triangles 32-33, 60

• D •

diagonal stitch 25
dressmakers' scissors 9

• E •

embroidery 12–19
    Beautiful buttons 20-21
    Felt flowers 16-17
    Pictures in stitches 18-19, 62
    techniques 13–15
embroidery hoops 12, 13
embroidery scissors 9
embroidery stitches
    back stitch 14
    blanket stitch 14
    chain stitch 14
    cross stitch 14
    crown stitch 15
    French knot 15
    running stitch 14
equipment and materials 8–9

• F •

fabrics
    cotton fabric 8
    even-weave fabrics 12, 13

for appliqué 36
for embroidery 12
for patchwork 28
plain-weave fabrics 12, 13
felt 8, 36
    Cup-cake bag 40-41
    Felt flowers 16-17
    Needle case 42-43
    Stripy pouch 26-27
flowers
    Felt flowers 16-17
    Knitted roses 52-53
French knot 15

• G •

gadget pouch 27
greeting cards 19

• I •

interlocking straight stitch 25

• K •

knitting 44-53
    casting off 49
    casting on 45
    ends, tidying 49
    joining new yarn 49
    Knitted roses 52-53
    knitting in new colour 49
    shaping 48
    techniques 45-51
    yarns 44
knitting needles 44
knitting spool 44
knitting stitches
    decreasing 48
    garter stitch 47

Acknowledgments

Dorling Kindersley would like to thank:
Gemma Fletcher and Rosie Levine for design
assistance; David Fentiman for editorial
assistance; Penny Arlon for proofreading;
Ray Williams for production help.

All images © Dorling Kindersley
For further information see:
www.dkimages.com